TINY THINGS BIG IMPACTS

PLANKTON

Written By John Wood

BookLife
PUBLISHING

©2018
BookLife Publishing
King's Lynn
Norfolk PE30 4LS

All rights reserved.
Printed in Malaysia.

A catalogue record for this
book is available from the
British Library.

ISBN: 978-1-78637-423-3

Written by:
John Wood

Edited by:
Kirsty Holmes

Designed by:
Amy Li

PLANKTON

CONTENTS:

WORDS THAT LOOK LIKE THIS ARE EXPLAINED IN THE GLOSSARY ON PAGE 31.

MEET THE PLANKTON

These are plankton. Plankton live in water, and they come in all sorts of different shapes and sizes. A lot of plankton are so small that they can only be seen through a **microscope**. However, even though they are tiny, plankton change the world every day. They might seem unimportant, but without them our lives would be very different indeed.

Plants and Animals

There are two different types of plankton. Phytoplankton (say: fi-toe-plank-tun) are like plants. They are often called algae. Zooplankton are animals. Most are too small to be seen, although some can grow quite big.

JELLYFISH ARE A TYPE OF ZOOPLANKTON.

Float On

Plankton are mostly carried around by ocean **currents**, rather than doing all the swimming themselves. Some plankton, such as jellyfish and other zooplankton, can swim up and down or push themselves forwards with a burst of air. However, most of their movement comes from the currents.

A Copepod under a Microscope

COPEPODS ARE A TYPE OF ZOOPLANKTON. THERE ARE MORE COPEPODS IN THE WORLD THAN THERE ARE INSECTS.

Algae on a Lake

Phytoplankton, or algae, mostly float on top of water, where there is more sunlight. Zooplankton can be found throughout the ocean, although most of them live near the top, eating the phytoplankton. Some animals begin life as zooplankton and change into something different later on. These are called meroplankton.

A WORLD WITHOUT PLANKTON

The Food Chain

A food chain shows what eats what in the animal world. Food chains start with something that makes the food. This is usually a plant. Plants are eaten by plant-eating animals, called herbivores. Animals that eat other animals are called carnivores.

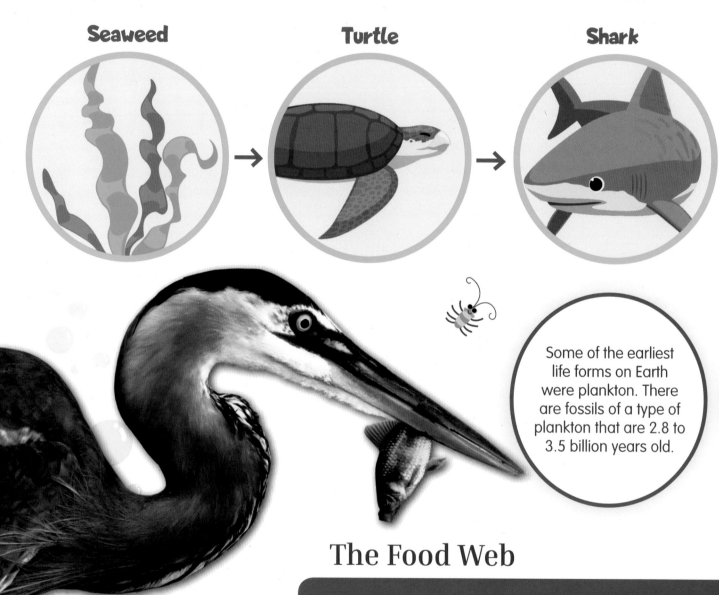

Seaweed → **Turtle** → **Shark**

Some of the earliest life forms on Earth were plankton. There are fossils of a type of plankton that are 2.8 to 3.5 billion years old.

The Food Web

If lots of food chains are joined up, a food web is created. This looks a lot more complicated. All animals, including humans, are connected by the world's food web. Any changes to one part of the web can affect other animals too.

Plankton in the Food Web

Phytoplankton are at the start of the food web for all animals who live in water. This means they are very important – without plankton, herbivores wouldn't have anything to eat. If the herbivores starved, then carnivores wouldn't have anything to eat either.

EVERYTHING THAT LIVES IN THE WATER NEEDS PLANKTON – EVEN THE BIGGER ANIMALS.

Parting With Plankton

If all the plankton disappeared tomorrow, nobody knows what would happen for sure. Maybe humans would find a way to replace plankton and solve all the problems. But what if we couldn't? Throughout this book, we are going to take a look at what might happen in a world without plankton.

WHALE

Daily News

Since 1928

LAST BLUE WHALE EATS EVERYTHING!

By J.Pointer

Since the plankton all disappeared, blue whales have had nothing to eat. After disappearing one by one, the last blue whale is now being kept alive by a nearby school cafeteria. The whale, nicknamed 'Fatty' by the children, eats a huge amount of fish. "We are going to run out of food!" said Emilie, the head dinner lady. "We need the plankton back!"

I interviewed one of the children walking by, and asked him his thoughts on the newest arrival to the primary school. "I love him. He is eating all the terrible school food. I'm surprised he hasn't been sick yet – all the other children have. I just don't wanna be around when the vomit comes."

After this encounter, I went to find the cook. After tracking the pungent, unmistakable scent of burnt carrots, the cook was discovered in the kitchen. "Fatty is eating all of the school food," she said.
More on page 14.

Whales and Plankton

Blue whales are the biggest animals ever to have lived on Earth. However, they eat very small animals – a type of zooplankton called krill.

KRILL ARE AROUND 5 CENTIMETRES (CM) LONG. BLUE WHALES ARE AROUND 30 METRES (M) LONG.

Blue whales do not have teeth. Instead the inside of their mouths are covered with **baleen plates**. This makes it easy to eat zooplankton, but difficult to eat much else. If plankton disappeared, even giant animals like blue whales wouldn't survive.

A blue whale's heart can weigh as much as a car.

Baleen Plates

Sometimes whales can eat over 3,600 kilograms (kg) of zooplankton a day.

Animal Lovers

Blue whales are beautiful and intelligent animals. They are the biggest animals on the planet, and they even sing whale songs underwater. Losing plankton means losing animals such as whales. This would make the world a lot less interesting indeed.

Krill

NO FISH
ON THE MENU

Green Hills Primary School
Tel: 636-555-3226
Email: info@greenhillsprimary.sch.uk

Dear Parent or Guardian,

I am writing this letter to tell you that there will be no more fish to eat at lunchtime. This is because all the fish have gone. Here is a list of changes to the lunchtime menu:

Tuesday: Instead of fish fingers, we will now have broccoli stew with extra broccoli.
Friday: Instead of fish and chips, we will now have Spinach Surprise.

Yours sincerely,

Ms Rippengill
Head Teacher

MANY FISH
EAT ALGAE.

Back to the Food Web

Everything is connected to the food web, even humans. No plankton means there will be no small fish. No small fish means that there won't be any big fish for humans to eat.

Fishing Boat

Fish Around the World

Humans eat a lot of fish. There are around 4.6 million fishing boats sailing around the world and catching fish. Some of those boats are very big, and catch a lot of fish. Without plankton, a lot of our food would be gone.

Fish are often cheaper than meat, so they are an important food for people who don't have a lot of money, especially in **less economically developed countries**. These countries sell a lot of fish around the world and make a lot of money. Without this money, people would be poorer.

Over 100 million tonnes of fish are eaten every year around the world.

HOLIDAYS

"HI GUYS, WELCOME TO MY CHANNEL! THIS WAS GOING TO BE A VIDEO ABOUT MY HOLIDAY AT THE GREAT BARRIER REEF WITH MY PARENTS, BUT THEY TOLD ME THAT IT'S GONE! APPARENTLY WHEN THOSE TINY PLANKTON – I THINK THAT'S WHAT THEY ARE CALLED – DISAPPEARED, SO DID A BUNCH OF OTHER STUFF!"

The biggest coral reef in the world is the Great Barrier Reef in Australia.

Coral Reefs

Without plankton, many beautiful parts of the world will also disappear. For example, coral reefs need plankton to survive.

Jobs and Money

Without coral reefs, or beautiful sea creatures, people would stop visiting some places in the world for their holidays. When people visit a place on holiday, it is called tourism. Tourism is good because people spend lots of money on holiday, and the places they visit get richer.

PLACES WITH CORAL REEFS HAVE LOTS OF VISITORS BECAUSE THEY ARE SO BEAUTIFUL.

Places like Australia and Fiji need tourism. A lot of their tourism comes from amazing things like coral reefs. Without tourism, lots of people could lose their jobs and have no money to look after themselves.

IT MIGHT SEEM SURPRISING, BUT MILLIONS OF JOBS DEPEND ON PLANKTON, AND ARE LOST WITHOUT THEM.

13

WORRIED DOCTORS

AND SICK PEOPLE

MEDICAL CENTRE

ATTENTION PATIENTS

Some of the medicines we use no longer work. Your doctor might not be able to treat some illnesses. We are very sorry.

The Problem with Old Medicine

When someone has an **infection**, doctors give them a type of medicine called an antibiotic. Antibiotics are used to treat all sorts of things, like ear and eye infections. Antibiotics kill **bacteria**, but some bacteria are changing and can't be destroyed. Doctors and scientists think that our antibiotics won't work forever. This means we need to find new ways of making antibiotics.

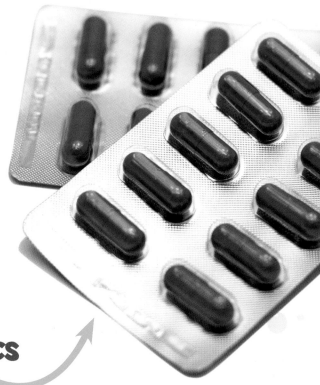

Antibiotics

A New Hope

So far, a lot of medicines and antibiotics have come from plants on land. Around 120 medicines in the world today come straight from rainforest plants.

THE AMAZON RAINFOREST IS THE BIGGEST RAINFOREST. IT CONTAINS AROUND 40,000 SPECIES OF PLANT.

However, scientists might find new types of medicine in the ocean. Corals, animals and life found in ocean trenches might help us to create new antibiotics. Scientists think that the new medicines will be able to kill the new bacteria. However, without plankton, no life would survive in the ocean, which would mean that no new medicines could be found.

Ocean trenches can be up to 11 kilometres (km) deep. Sunlight does not reach the bottom of the trenches.

Ocean Trench

SO CLOSE TO A CURE

tweeter

⚙ 👤 FOLLOW

Professor Tess Tube
@Bensonrules

No! We were SO CLOSE to finding a cure! All we needed was a little longer to study the coral reefs... If anyone needs me, I'll be at home with a bucket of ice cream, feeling sad.
#ComeBackPlankton #AlgaeSavesLives
#MaybeIWillHaveTwoBuckets

223,958,022 Retweets   **824,223** Likes

 Reply to @Bensonrules

Under the Sea

Scientists now think that the cures to all kinds of illnesses might be found in the ocean. Unlike on land, not many people have explored the ocean for medicine. Although these cures might not come from plankton, they will definitely come from creatures that need plankton to survive.

Humans have only explored 5% of the ocean.

Sea Sponges

Some illnesses, like **cancer**, can be very serious. Although there are ways to treat cancer, scientists are always looking for even better medicines. Some of these medicines have been found in sea sponges. Sea sponges are creatures that live throughout the ocean, and they contain **chemicals** which have already been used in cancer medicines. There may be even more useful chemicals to find.

What Do Sea Sponges Eat?

Sea sponges mostly eat algae, or other microscopic plankton. They would not survive if the plankton disappeared, and we would not find cancer medicine if the sea sponges did not survive.

Some sea sponges measure less than 2 cm, while others can be more than 3 m wide.

Sea Sponge

SEA SPONGES CAN GROW BACK PIECES OF THEMSELVES THAT HAVE BROKEN OFF.

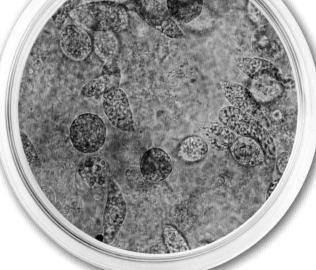

EXTREME WEATHER

Your Local Weather
Friday, April 23, 2024

9:41   100%

Heavy Snow

9°

Sat		5°	0°
Sun		18°	9°
Mon		10°	5°
Tue		24°	21°
Wed		20°	16°
Thu		16°	8°

Climate Change

Humans do a lot of things that aren't good for the **environment**. When we burn **fossil fuels** to make electricity or to fuel cars or planes, a gas called carbon dioxide is released into the air. Carbon dioxide causes more heat to be trapped on Earth, which can change the weather (or climate) all around the world. This is called climate change.

CLIMATE CHANGE CAN LEAD TO MORE EXTREME WEATHER IN SOME PARTS OF THE WORLD, LIKE HURRICANES AND FLOODS.

Carbon Underwater

A lot of carbon is stored in the oceans. This is because phytoplankton take in carbon, water and sunlight and use these things to make energy. Dead plankton, and dead animals which have eaten plankton, sink to the bottom of the ocean. The carbon is stored in the ocean until it naturally rises.

THE WORLD'S PHYTOPLANKTON TAKE UP A LOT LESS ROOM THAN THE WORLD'S PLANTS. HOWEVER, PHYTOPLANKTON TAKE IN 40% OF THE CARBON.

When tiny bits of living things sink to the ocean floor, it is sometimes called marine snow.

There would be much more carbon in the air if it weren't for plankton. This means climate change would be much worse. There would be more hurricanes, floods, storms and droughts. This would make life very hard for every animal on land, including humans.

Algae under a Microscope

CLOUD
CONTROL

"LOOKING OUT OVER THE OCEANS, IT LOOKS LIKE IT IS GOING TO BE CLEAR TODAY, TOMORROW, THE DAY AFTER THAT AND... WHY ARE THERE SO FEW CLOUDS OVER THE SEA NOW? THERE MUST BE SOMETHING MISSING FROM THE OCEAN. WHAT PLANTS OR ANIMALS IN THE OCEAN COULD BE THAT IMPORTANT?"

The Answer is Always Plankton

Plankton help create clouds over the ocean. Clouds are made up of tiny droplets of water that stick to **particles**. When enough of these droplets get together, a cloud is formed.

Albedo

Albedo is the amount of sunlight that the Earth reflects. Some things reflect a lot of sunlight, like fluffy white clouds, or the snowy North and South Poles. Other things don't reflect as much sunlight, like the oceans and forests.

The amount of sunlight reflected by an ocean cloud depends on how many particles and droplets it is made up of.

Cooling Down

Reflecting or blocking sunlight is a good thing because it keeps the planet cooler. A cooler planet means the climate probably won't change as much. This means that plankton are also helping keep the weather safe and normal by helping to create clouds.

ALTHOUGH PLANKTON HELP KEEP THE EARTH COOL, THEY CAN'T ALWAYS KEEP UP WITH WHAT HUMANS DO TO THE ENVIRONMENT.

THE EARTH
GETS OUT OF BREATH

"T-THIS IS ... THE NEWS. OUR... OUR TOP STORY TONIGHT IS... SORRY, I'M A BIT OUT OF BREATH. NO ... REALLY, THAT IS THE TOP STORY. SINCE... THE PLANKTON DISAPPEARED, THERE... ISN'T MUCH... AIR THAT WE CAN BREATHE. OK... IT IS TIME FOR THE WEATHER... I'M GOING TO GO AND LIE DOWN."

BREAKING NEWS

BREAKING NEWS
LIVE NEWS
WHERE'S THE AIR?
GLOBAL OXYGEN OUTAGE

What Do You Need to Survive?

There are a few things that every human needs in order to survive. Everyone needs food, sleep, water and oxygen. Oxygen is all around us in the air that we breathe. But where does it come from?

The Carbon Cycle

Oxygen is released by plants and plankton. Humans and animals breathe oxygen in, and breathe out carbon dioxide. Plants and plankton take in carbon dioxide, as well as sunlight and water, to give them the energy that they need to survive. Then it happens all over again. This is called the carbon cycle.

The Carbon Cycle

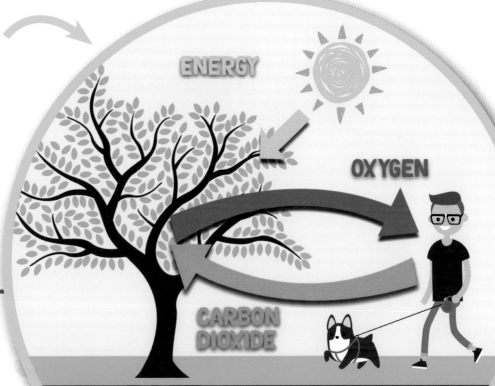

Plankton create half of the oxygen that we breathe.

The carbon cycle shows how different forms of life work together. Animals and plants need each other to survive. The oxygen that plankton release is especially important for the animals in the sea, but it affects humans too.

A WORLD WITH TOO MUCH PLANKTON

BREAKING NEWS

STAY AWAY FROM RIVERS, LAKES AND OCEANS.

A huge number of plankton have appeared from nowhere! These areas of water are now quite dangerous. Do not eat anything that has recently come from the nearby oceans. A full story will be released soon.

SOME ALGAE BLOOMS CAN BE SEEN FROM SPACE.

Blooms can be green, yellow, or red.

The Dark Side of Plankton

When lots of new algae appear, it is called a bloom. In a bloom there can be hundreds or even thousands of algae **cells** in every millilitre of water. However, if there is too much plankton, this can be harmful to everything in the water.

The Red Tide

Red tides are out-of-control blooms of certain types of plankton. Some red tides can be harmful. The plankton may release **toxins,** which are dangerous to the other animals in the water. If people catch and eat animals that have eaten toxins, it is dangerous for the people too. It can also be difficult to breathe in the air around the bloom.

When lots of algae die and **rot**, it uses up a lot of oxygen in the water. This is bad for the other animals, as they might not have enough oxygen to live.

RED TIDES ARE ALSO CALLED HARMFUL ALGAL BLOOMS (HABS).

The same type of plankton that causes red tides can also glow in the dark sometimes.

THREATS

TO PLANKTON

Northern Hemisphere

A world without plankton looks scary indeed. However, in the real world plankton are in danger.

After studying plankton, scientists have found that there is less plankton in all of the oceans than there was 20 years ago. This is especially true in the Northern Hemisphere. There are many reasons why there is less plankton around the world today.

> A WARMER WORLD IS CAUSED BY HOW HUMANS LIVE.

Climate Change

As the world gets warmer, scientists think this might be affecting plankton. Warmer water in the ocean doesn't mix with the colder water underneath, which contains **nutrients**. This makes it harder for plankton to grow and survive.

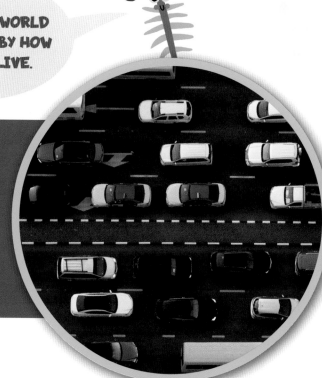

Warmer waters might force plankton to be closer to the North and South Poles. This is because the temperature would be lower in these areas, and they would find it easier to survive.

IF PLANKTON MOVED AROUND THE WORLD, IT WOULD ALSO CHANGE WHERE OTHER ANIMALS WOULD LIVE.

Some plankton like **acidic** water, but many do not.

Acid Ocean

Because humans are creating so much carbon dioxide, the ocean is taking in more and more carbon. This makes the water more acidic. Plankton need to have the water just right – if the water was too acidic, many plankton would die out.

Plastic

Many people know that plastic in the ocean can be dangerous for animals. Sea turtles swallow plastic bags because they think they are jellyfish, and this is very harmful. However, plankton can also swallow very tiny bits of plastic, which can kill them.

MANY ANIMALS THINK THE PLASTIC IS FOOD.

There are around 51 trillion particles of plastic in oceans all over the world.

Humans dump a lot of rubbish in the sea, including plastic. If this carries on, it may be very harmful to ocean life. It is important that people recycle plastic, and companies cut down on the amount of plastic that they use.

MOST PLASTIC DOESN'T BREAK DOWN FOR HUNDREDS OF YEARS.

Do Humans Cause Red Tides?

Nobody is exactly sure what causes red tides. Extreme weather may be one cause, while wind and water currents could be another. Many people think that humans sometimes cause them too, when extra nutrients flow into the water from lawns and farmland.

Chinese Farmland

Is There One Reason?

Plankton have a lot of things to deal with. There probably isn't one single reason why plankton are disappearing – it is probably lots of reasons all added up. However, there are things being done to save plankton and the rest of the environment.

Orange Nettle Jellyfish

SAVING
THE PLANKTON

Although climate change is still a problem, humans have done many good things for the environment. For example, the Paris Climate Agreement is an agreement between countries to release less carbon dioxide into the air.

Things like solar panels and wind turbines create electricity in a way that is friendly to the environment. This is called green energy, and it is more popular than ever.

What Can You Do to Help?

- Recycle your rubbish. Ask an adult what can be recycled.

- To save electricity, turn off things like lights and televisions when you are not using them. You could also ask your parents if they are using energy-saving bulbs.

- Talk about plankton! Tell everyone that they are one of the most important tiny things in the world.

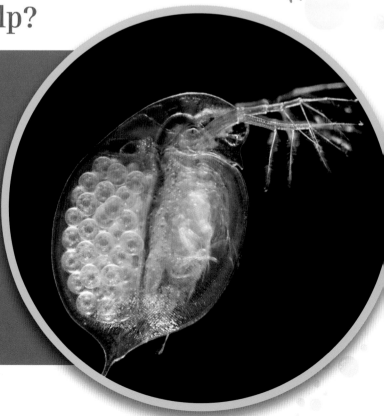

GLOSSARY

acidic	contains a chemical substance that causes damage to the natural environment
bacteria	microscopic living things that can cause diseases
baleen plates	the part of a whale's mouth that is used for filtering
cancer	a serious disease caused by the uncontrolled dividing of cells
cells	the basic units that make up all living things
chemicals	substances that materials are made from
currents	steady flows of water in one direction
environment	the natural world
fossil fuels	fuels, such as coal, oil and gas, that formed millions of years ago from the remains of animals and plants
infection	an illness caused by dirt, germs and bacteria getting into the body
less economically developed countries	countries whose business, finance and manufacturing are not as strong as developed countries.
microscope	an instrument used by scientists to see very small things
nutrients	natural substances that plants and animals need to grow and stay healthy
particles	extremely small pieces of a substance
rot	spoil and break down
toxins	poisonous substances

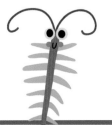

INDEX

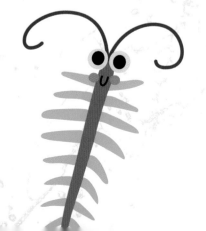